Saturday:
   8:30 Charity Gala (need tickets ??)

☐ Monday: Interview for a new
   assistant all morning (*be *underline*nice*!)

☐ 12 pm : Exercise!
   (yoga, spinning, or kick-boxing ?)

7:30 pm : Meet with vocal coach

Fashion Show in Brooklyn (need
       Wed. night manicure!)

☐ Recording session @ 1 pm. Wed!

Meet the girls for champagne
           Thurs. afternoon

Friday : Dinner Party (no fights
       @ 7:00 pm tonight !!)

Don't forget! Start writing new book!

☐ Call stripper for bachelorette party

   Turtle Time! @ 7 pm

"I ALWAYS TELL IT LIKE IT IS." —*NeNe*

theReal Housewives

TELL IT LIKE IT IS

Orange County · **New York City** · **Atlanta** · **New Jersey** · **D.C.** · **Beverly Hills** · **Miami**

 CHRONICLE BOOKS

 Bravo media

 MELCHER MEDIA

Library of Congress Cataloging-in-Publication Data

The real housewives tell it like it is : Orange County, New York City,
Atlanta, New Jersey, D.C., Beverly Hills, Miami.
p. cm.
ISBN 978-0-8118-7417-5
1. Real housewives television programs—Miscellanea. 2. Quotations,
American. I. Chronicle Books (Firm)
PN1992.8.R37R32 2011
791.45—dc22
2011015305

Manufactured in China

Designed by Paul Kepple and Ralph Geroni at Headcase Design.
Original text by Mimi O'Connor.

Produced by Melcher Media
124 West 13th Street, New York, New York 10011
www.melcher.com

1 3 5 7 9 10 8 6 4 2

Chronicle Books LLC
680 Second Street, San Francisco, California 94107
www.chroniclebooks.com

THE REAL HOUSEWIVES
TELL IT LIKE IT IS

6

Meet the
Housewives

15

CHAPTER ONE

Pearls of Wisdom

39

CHAPTER TWO

On How to Be a
Yummy Mummy

55

CHAPTER THREE

How to Entertain:

A Guide to Ladylike
Party Planning

75

CHAPTER FOUR

The Mind-Body
Connection:

Food, Heath, and Fitness

97

CHAPTER FIVE

The Quest for
Finding and Holding
On to Love

113

CHAPTER SIX

Doing It Ourselves:

Matters of Working,
Business, and Finance

129

CHAPTER SEVEN

Zen and the
Art of Conflict
Resolution

149

CHAPTER EIGHT

The Glamorous Life:

Fashion, Beauty, and the
Lengths We'll Go

175

The Golden Stiletto
Awards:

The Finest Achievements
in Saying, Wearing,
and Doing It in
Real Housewives Style

181

Test Your
Housewives IQ
with the Following
Quizzes

198

Credits and
Acknowledgments

Meet the Housewives

As the saying goes, it's not what you know—it's who you know. And if you don't know the Real Housewives, your social network needs a serious status update. Whether you like your ladies southern and sassy, edgy and urban, or with just a dash of Cali cool, there's a Housewife for you. Like a Jersey Girl? Fuhgeddaboudit, they're here. More of a politico? The wives are inside the Beltway. Perhaps you're a sucker for a woman who really knows how to spice things up—you must meet the women of Miami. But here's what: No matter where a Real Housewife calls home, she's guaranteed to be unforgettable. What's not to love?

TAMRA BARNEY   Orange County

"I'm the hottest Housewife in Orange County."

MANTRA:

ALEXIS BELLINO

Orange County

MANTRA:

"Am I high maintenance? Of course I am. Look at me!"

LYNNE CURTIN

Orange County

MANTRA:

"I am just your typical Orange County housewife. I am obsessed with being young."

VICKI GUNVALSON

Orange County

MANTRA:

"I want the power and the money, and I want them both."

JEANA KEOUGH

Orange County

MANTRA:

"It doesn't matter what happens in life; I do it my way."

LAURI WARING PETERSON

Orange County

MANTRA:

"You know what? I'm living the O.C. lifestyle again. I feel like royalty."

GRETCHEN ROSSI

Orange County

MANTRA:

"I love the bling, I love the jewelry, I love it all."

KELLY KILLOREN BENSIMON

New York City

MANTRA:

"I've created a great life, and I love living it."

LUANN DE LESSEPS

New York City

MANTRA:

"I never feel guilty about being privileged."

BETHENNY FRANKEL

New York City

MANTRA:

"New York City is my playground."

ALEX MCCORD

New York City

MANTRA:

"To a certain group of people in New York, status is everything."

SONJA MORGAN

New York City

MANTRA:

"I have a taste for luxury, and luxury has a taste for me."

RAMONA SINGER

New York City

MANTRA:

"I like making my own money. I find that an aphrodisiac."

JILL ZARIN

"I run with a fabulous circle of people."

MANTRA:

CYNTHIA BAILEY

Atlanta

"I know how to work it and be seen."

MANTRA:

KANDI BURRUSS

Atlanta

"I'm an independent woman doing it for myself."

MANTRA:

LISA WU HARTWELL

Atlanta

"If it doesn't make me money, I don't do it."

MANTRA:

NENE LEAKES

Atlanta

"When I walk into a room, I own it."

MANTRA:

PHAEDRA PARKS

Atlanta

"I'm the ultimate Southern belle. I get what I want."

MANTRA:

SHEREE WHITFIELD

Atlanta

MANTRA:

"People are intimidated by my success."

KIM ZOLCIAK

Atlanta

MANTRA:

"People call me a gold digger, but they just want what I have."

TERESA GIUDICE

New Jersey

MANTRA:

"People make fun of Jersey girls, but I think they're just jealous."

JACQUELINE LAURITA

New Jersey

MANTRA:

"Everyone likes to have nice things, but I'm not one to brag about it."

CAROLINE MANZO

New Jersey

MANTRA:

"If you're gonna mess with my family, you mess with me."

DINA MANZO

New Jersey

MANTRA:

"If you think I'm a bitch, then bring it on."

DANIELLE STAUB

New Jersey

MANTRA:

"You're either going to love me or hate me.
There is no in between with me."

MARY SCHMIDT AMONS

D.C.

MANTRA:

"I don't make money; I spend money."

LYNDA ERKILETIAN

D.C.

MANTRA:

"I give people enough rope to hang themselves,
and the smart people don't."

CAT OMMANNEY

D.C.

MANTRA:

"I'm here for a good time, not a long time."

MICHAELE SALAHI

D.C.

MANTRA:

"People have a hard time saying no to me, and that's
just been my blessing."

STACIE SCOTT TURNER

D.C.

MANTRA:

"D.C. is my town, and I thrive in it."

TAYLOR ARMSTRONG

Beverly Hills

MANTRA:

"It may look like I have it all, but I want more."

CAMILLE GRAMMER

Beverly Hills

MANTRA:

"It's time for me to come out of my husband's shadow and shine."

ADRIENNE MALOOF

Beverly Hills

MANTRA:

"Money is what I have, not who I am."

KIM RICHARDS

Beverly Hills

MANTRA:

"I was a child star, but now my most important role is being a mother."

KYLE RICHARDS

Beverly Hills

MANTRA:

"In a town full of phonies, I'm not afraid to be me."

LISA VANDERPUMP

Beverly Hills

MANTRA:

"In Beverly Hills, it's who you know, and I know everyone."

LEA BLACK

Miami

"I care about a lot of things. What others think of me isn't one of them."

MANTRA:

ADRIANA DE MOURA

Miami

"I speak five languages, but I can get a man with no words."

MANTRA:

ALEXIA ECHEVARRIA

Miami

"Beauty is power if you know how to use it."

MANTRA:

MARYSOL PATTON

Miami

"I put others in the spotlight, but somehow it keeps finding me."

MANTRA:

LARSA PIPPEN

Miami

"My husband's got moves, but I run the game."

MANTRA:

CRISTY RICE

Miami

"In my world, attitude is everything. I'm keeping it real."

MANTRA:

Chapter One

PEARLS

of

WISDOM

"Close your legs to married men."

 NENE

"I have all the beauty secrets. I will share with you . . . spend money."

 RAMONA

"Let
your haters
be your
motivators."

 SHEREE

"Just pretend you're on the phone. It really **pisses people off.**"

DANIELLE

(on avoiding talking to Teresa and Jacqueline at the Posche fashion show)

"Who gonna check me, **Boo?**"

 SHEREE

"Did I ever flip a table before that time?
No, I didn't. Will I ever flip another table?
I'm not sure."

 TERESA

"Who wants to die tomorrow and say, 'I haven't had a one-night stand'? Seriously."

 SONJA

"Oh my God, I forgot to Twitter."

🍎 | **JILL**

"You're just like a tutu! Tutu foo foo!"

🍎 | **RAMONA** *(to Simon on the dance floor)*

(23)

not so bad!" —RAMONA

"Ohmygod. Ohmygod. Ohmygod. Dear God. This is not good."

KYLE
(upon seeing naked photos of Camille)

"Holy mother of balls!"

TAMRA

"Oh my God!
Al Sharpton!
Al Sharpton!"

KELLY

(mistaking Bethenny's Jack Nicholson impression on Scary Island)

"If you can't feel, then you're dead, Kelly."

 RAMONA

"I'm feeling James Brown."

 LUANN

"Oh my God, I feel like such a pimp!"

TAMRA *(upon receiving her diamond-studded Rolex)*

"I'm a conversation piece."

KIM

"I don't know
if I can spend
a summer
or a year in
**this confined
space.**"

 CAMILLE
(on her 3,500-square-foot New York apartment)

"'Darling' is my favorite word, and I'm not giving it up for anyone."

LUANN

"I don't talk shit.
I talk the truth."

TAMRA

"'Bitch' means beautiful.
That's what that means to me."

KIM

But Occasionally Hold Your Tongue

"Keep it cute or put it on mute!"

CYNTHIA

"Usually I'm the one doing all the talking.
These two girls are out-yenta-ing me."

JILL *(on LuAnn and Sonja's gossiping)*

"I've never been
speechless.
I'm speechless."

RAMONA *(on Jill's surprise arrival on Scary Island)*

"I could see the smokestacks burning, but nothing's coming out of her mouth."

🍎 **JILL** *(on Alex trying to deliver her message)*

"I can't talk to you;
you have

🍎 **RAMONA**

Chapter Two

On How to Be a

YUMMY
MUMMY

"Seriously.

I'll take your car,
I'll take your phone,
I'll take your life.

Well, I won't take your life,
but I'll take your car
and your phone."

VICKI *(to her daughter Brianna)*

"I don't want you guys **playing with fire** while I'm gone."

🍎 | LUANN *(to her children)*

"Well, I do have a chapter in the book called

'Don't Listen to the Well-Meaning Morons.'"

 **ALEX** *(on Jill)*

"I cannot be screaming like a wolf and poopin' on no tables."

 PHAEDRA *(on her need for drugs during childbirth)*

"I *am* the **best mom in the world.**"

 DANIELLE

"Four years old
is the age that I think
a little girl should
get her first
special piece
of jewelry."

TAYLOR

"Holy shitballs! I'm pregnant!"

 BETHENNY

"I'm your mommy. I can't wait to dress you up."

TERESA *(to her day-old baby girl Audriana)*

"We need to get you a **bling-bling pacifier**."

TERESA *(to her newborn Audriana)*

"This is going to sound crazy. **Don't judge me.** I have four nannies, and they rotate."

CAMILLE

Be Supportive of Your Friends' Families

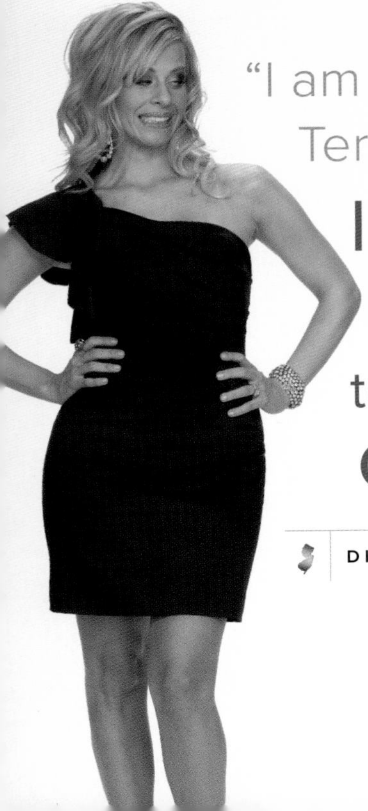

"I am not delivering Teresa's baby. I have no desire to see her chucky."

DINA

"Unless she wants one of **the Village People,** I think she's better off having a little girl."

 DINA *(on Teresa)*

"Grandma Wrinkles is nasty."

 CAROLINE *(on Dina's cat)*

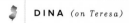

"It looks like it's not real. It runs on batteries or something."

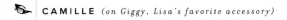

CAMILLE *(on Giggy, Lisa's favorite accessory)*

Chapter Three

HOW TO ENTERTAIN:

A Guide to

Ladylike Party  *Planning*

What Makes a Successful Party?

"I'm always tardy for my own party."

🍎 SONJA

"I've always wanted a Louis Vuitton birthday cake."

🍎 SHEREE

"This is the best dinner party I've ever had, because the lunatic came out. Wow!"

🍎 BETHENNY

"It ain't a party until Ramona gets loaded."

BETHENNY

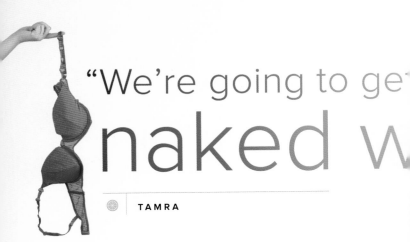

"We're going to ge
naked w

TAMRA

Gretchen

asted."

"Women + alcohol + a pole equals a great time."

 **SHEREE** *(on a pole-dancing party)*

"Ramona's having fun, though. She's renewing her vows, she's renewing her buzz, she's renewing her life."

BETHENNY *(on Ramona during her renewal getaway)*

"When we get drunk, it's all about the boobs."

TAMRA

"Cheers to
being real."

KIM

"Cheers to
not being
fake."

VICKI

"Here's to
all the
gold
diggers."

  NENE

"Here's to hoping my boob doesn't fall out."

 KYLE

"Cheers to us. Cheers to skinny bitches."

TAMRA

"Here's to a crazy bunch of girlfriends."

VICKI

"Thank you so much, but

the Countess

doesn't drink

from a bottle."

 LUANN *(declining a beer at a party)*

"I know you're American, but let's have some manners."

CAT

"There's never a bad day to take your clothes off."

 DANIELLE

"Here's a tip. Here would be good manners: Mind your beeswax."

BETHENNY
(on LuAnn)

"To say anything inappropriate in front of strangers, that's so Ramona."

KELLY

Relax and Enjoy, but Remember the Potency of Potables

"That's a woo-hoo drink."

VICKI

"She calls me the buzzkill. Nobody could kill that buzz."

LUANN *(on Ramona's bachelorette partying)*

"This moment makes me realize that **the Prozac** and the **margaritas** were so smart."

BETHENNY *(during fashion week)*

"Stoner? No way. Not me. No way."

LYNNE

"I'm on **no crack pipe.**"

🍎 **RAMONA** *(on her unpredictable behavior)*

"After my incident with Kelly, I wanna suck the buzz out of Ramona's veins. I want a contact high. Honestly. I want to vampire her ass and get some of that Pinot Grigio in my system."

🍎 **BETHENNY**

Chapter Four

The
MIND-BODY CONNECTION:

Food, Health, and Fitness

Consider That
You Are What You Eat

"I'm starving.

KIM

I need a drink."

"I don't eat processed foods. I actually like **Gummi Bears.**"

KELLY

"Gummi Bears don't come from the vine.
Those aren't the bears you see in the Bronx Zoo."

BETHENNY
(on Kelly's contradictory eating habits)

"Anyone want a jelly bean?"

KELLY

"I wonder if it was a pet beforehand.
I don't wanna eat anything that has a name.
You know, like Bambi . . ."

 LEA

"I'm gonna tell you
the **real secret**
to the man's heart, and
**it ain't his
stomach, OK?"**

 NENE

"That's my chicken.
That's my chicken.
Ya know,
gimme that
chicken."

 KIM

*(on winning the fight with
Single Gary over the last
chicken at the market)*

"It wasn't a breakdown; it was a breakthrough."

 KELLY

"You seriously have mad cow."

 TAMRA

"Diarrhea of the mouth is not a real ailment."

 BETHENNY

"When [she] was going off on me, it was like a **mental institution** without **medication**."

DANIELLE *(on Teresa)*

"Adios, lunatics. I'm going over to the Hooters boat so I can meet some sane people."

BETHENNY

"The girl is **freakin'**
obsessed with me.
I don't know if she
wants to be me or
skin me and
wear me like last
year's Versace."

DINA *(on Danielle)*

"I thought I had a stroke,

but it was my false eyelashes making one eye smaller than the other."

 KYLE

"I'm very afraid of Lynne with a knife. I'm afraid of Lynne without a knife."

 TAMRA

"I've always been attracted to people who are missing a few screws. You're not normal unless you're missing a few screws."

MARYSOL

Feeling Good Is the First Step to Looking Good

"Just because someone is a model does not mean that they're **gorgeous.** That just means they're **skinny and tall** and can **wear a size two or zero.**"

 PHAEDRA

"They were like, 'Mom, you look great. It's all good.'...And it's a good image for them to be healthy and fit."

 KELLY *(on her kids and her Playboy shoot)*

"Oh my GOD, I'm good-looking."

 KIM

"I don't see myself as a beauty queen. I see myself more like Miss Universe."

 ALEXIA

"It would have been much easier not to have such

enormous aspirations.

It's a lot of pressure."

TAYLOR

"I'm a free bitch! Woo!"

TAMRA *(on her divorce)*

"I'm gonna take the high road, 'cause at the end of the day, I am a grown-ass woman."

SHEREE

"What happened was, I'm way too nice of a person and way too real and way too authentic."

 **KELLY** *(on her arrest)*

"I'm a **black woman** trapped in a **white woman's body.**"

 KIM

"I'm really the most approachable, down-to-earth person. Which most people don't get."

 LUANN

"I'm so shy.
I'm like, … deathly shy."

CAMILLE

Chapter Five

The Quest for

FINDING and **HOLDING ON**

to

LOVE

"I honestly believe everybody should be for lease.

It's like a car. There might be something new that comes along."

GRETCHEN

"It just seems like he has a history of
serial Housewife dating."

LAURI *(to Gretchen on her choice to date Slade)*

"Men always wanted to marry me."

 RAMONA

"The rock was so big, I was like, HELL to the YEAH!"

 KIM
*(on her engagement ring
from Big Poppa)*

"Seventeen years is not a milestone. I mean, **being married to her every day is a milestone,** to be honest."

🍎 **JILL**
(on Ramona's decision to renew her vows)

"I was kind of like Rapunzel. You know, I was kind of, like, stuck in the castle in the Hamptons. I wanna be Robin to Batman."

🍎 **KELLY** *(on married life)*

"I think Joe and I are a little bit old-fashioned,
but in a cute way. We have sex every day.
Sometimes twice!"

 TERESA

"I say to him, 'You know what?

Christmas
and birthdays.

And that's your

birthday, not mine—

that's another day off.'"

 LISA *(on sex with her husband)*

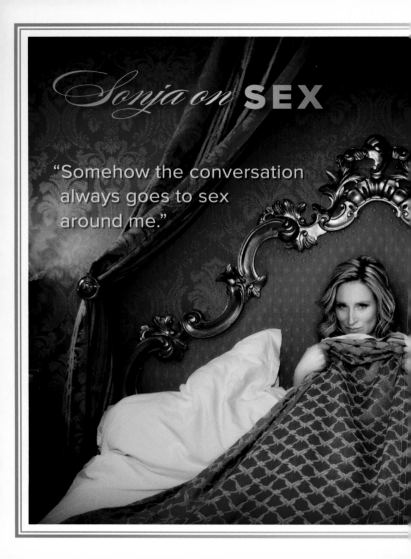

Sonja on **SEX**

"Somehow the conversation always goes to sex around me."

On sex as a divorcée:

"I mean, until you get married again,
what are you supposed to do,
put it on the shelf?"

"Just because you're divorced,
you're not dead. Having
regular sex is so important."

"I think I go very well with men."

*On the pros and cons of sleeping
with a well-endowed man:*

"It doesn't matter, but it doesn't
hurt to have a little extra.
Well, maybe it does hurt."

"Are you guys going to make out with

KELLY
*(to Bethenny
and Ramona on
Scary Island)*

the tongue?"

"I'm gonna look like a loose girl, but then I thought,
'You know what? Everybody seems to be doing it.'"

ADRIANA
*(on taking pole-dancing lessons to
spice up her love life with her boyfriend)*

"I believe the only safe way to have sex is abstinence."

DANIELLE

dynamite there was only a two-inch fuse."

Chapter Six

DOING IT OURSELVES:

Matters of
Working, Business, and Finance

Always Know How to Support Yourself

"Rosa is my angel—who just happens to be my housekeeper. If I had to do what Rosa does every day, I wouldn't be able to do anything except clean this house."

 MARY

"She thinks I owe her an apology. Good thing she don't get paid for thinking."

 KANDI *(on her fight with NeNe)*

"Get a job, girlfriend.
Get a job.
You're not
too pretty
to work."

TERESA *(on Danielle and her financial situation)*

COUNTESS

"I'm not Madonna, but I could be

the female Barry White."

 LUANN
(on her budding career as a recording artist)

LUANN

MONEY CAN'T BUY YOU CLASS

Contains the **HIT SINGLE**
"CHIC, C'EST LA VIE"

also includes
"Oh, Darling" and "I Love That You Love Me"

"Well, I might consider
doing *Playboy*.
I was married to a European, so
being topless
is not that
big of a deal."

LUANN

"I mean, she really owns the town. I mean, **she actually does own** the town."

 LISA *(on being with Adrienne in Vegas)*

"What is she gonna do with a check? Like, stick it in her bra?"

 CRISTY

"Budget. What's that?

I don't shop on a budget."

 SHEREE

"I think the **conveniences** of being able to have people do things for you is really what **money means to me.**"

TAYLOR

"I wonder if she pays less because they use less fabric."

JILL *(on Kelly's very short dress)*

"She should ask
for a discount
because
it's like half
a dress."

LUANN *(on Kelly's very short dress)*

"32,000 dollars
for a gold necklace
really isn't that
expensive."

 KIM

"They turned up in this horrible white limo, which only my daughters would be impressed by—because they're nine!"

 CAT

"Kelsey and I have been flying private for years.

Until recently. Now we're taking more commercial.

So, you know, we try to be green."

 CAMILLE

"I want to download it on my phone like everyone else, but I haven't figured out how to do that yet."

🍎 **SONJA** *(on buying LuAnn's single)*

"I didn't put myself all over the Internet."

GRETCHEN

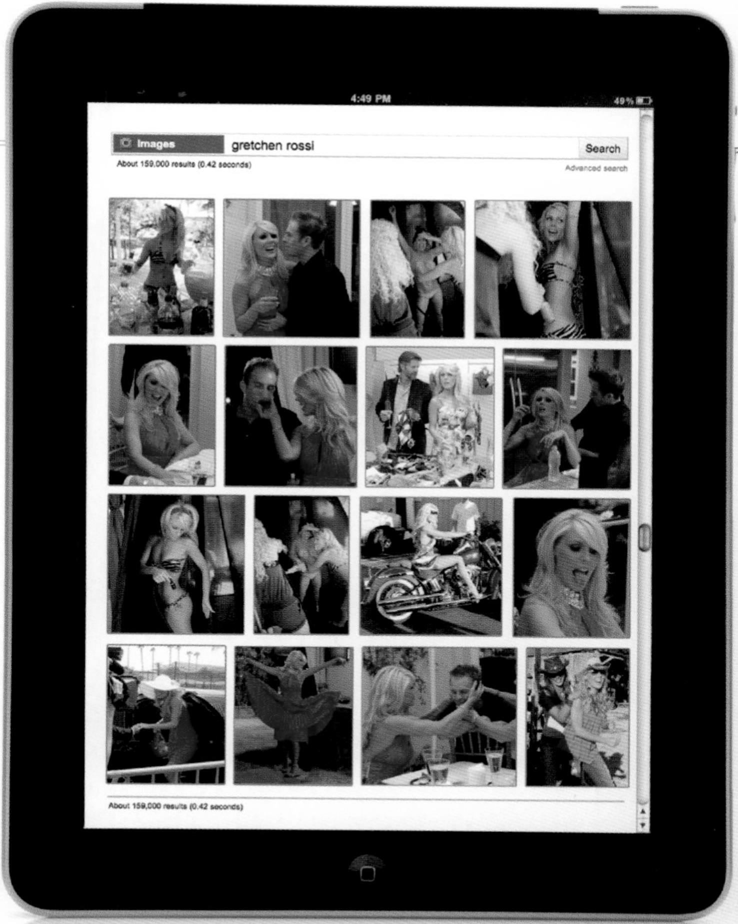

Chapter Seven

and the Art of

CONFLICT
RESOLUTION

"I'm not a villain. I'm not a beater-upper."

VICKI

"The person that remains in control is the one that wins."

 CAMILLE

"I'm really not a confrontational person."

 DANIELLE

"I'm gonna stop
    talking to you right
now, before I get
**blowing up
    on your ass."**

KANDI *(to NeNe)*

"Are we, like, brawling?
Like, where do we live,
Jersey?"

ALEXIS

"If you want to deflate an attack?
You always compliment."

KELLY

"You are in
high school.
You are a mean girl,
and you are in high school.
And while you are
in high school,
I am in
Brooklyn."

ALEX

"You guys
are making
**lemons into
lemonade...**
You're making
something into
something bigger."

KELLY

"I'm gonna get my Brooklyn on, and I'm gonna friggin' knock her block off."

 DINA *(on Danielle)*

"I'm getting crunk about it."

 NENE *(to Kandi)*

"I can barely
hold it together
to not
bitch-slap her."

 JILL

Oklahoma

"I'll flip you over the couch."

 LISA *(to Kim, at the season one reunion)*

"I'm about to take you out back and pull some on your ass."

 TAYLOR

"She can't change the

ho-bag

that she is."

 TERESA *(on Danielle)*

"Who uses the word
'ho-bag' these days?"

 LUANN

"I know who I am. I know

I'm not
a whore

or a **prostitute**

or a

cokehead."

 DANIELLE
(on Teresa's accusations)

whore!" —TERESA

Let the Healing Begin

"I will never forgive her for that. I might forget, though, because I forget everything, but I will never forgive her for that."

 **JILL** *(on Alex "delivering her message")*

"I don't think I got the **'Ramona and Simon Sittin' in a Tree'** memo."

BETHENNY

(on the surprising new friendship between her two castmates)

"I made a deposit in that friendship bank. And I feel like she **took the money and ran.** I feel like she cleared out our bank account."

JILL *(on her relationship with Bethenny)*

Chapter Eight

The

GLAMOROUS
LIFE:

*Fashion, Beauty, and the
Lengths We'll Go*

"I have to have
at least
three outfits a day,
and I have to
have backups."

 KYLE *(on her packing strategy)*

"She has the body
of a fashion model.
Maybe not
the face."

JILL

"This is the party, evidently, that we were all told to wear a square of toilet paper and make an outfit out of it.... It was like a yard sale of body parts."

 BETHENNY

"Mommy's gonna die in Dior."

 **KIM** *(to her daughter)*

"It's always a fashion show. It's Jersey, baby."

 DANIELLE

"Shoulders are the new boobs."

🍎 KELLY

"I gotta be honest. Simon has the worst taste."

🍎 KELLY

"I'm not abusing animals;
I'm just wea

🍎 KELLY

ring fur."

"When I walk in, all eyes on me. Ohhh. Wow. Bam! NeNe's in the house!"

 NENE *(on arriving at Sheree's birthday party)*

"You have to find the
perfect balance of
taking care of yourself
**and being
self-absorbed."**

ALEXIS

"I don't think you can ever have enough mirrors."

KIM

"Lashes poppin', lips bustin."

NENE
(preparing
to go out)

"She looked like she does every day. She certainly didn't look like she just pushed a **watermelon** out of **her chuckarella.**"

 DINA *(on Teresa postpartum)*

"Listen, we made history. Like, we brought glam to the farm, OK? This farm has never seen so much glam in its life. So today is history."

 CRISTY

"I'm this beautiful Barbie doll."

 KIM

"People call me the Cuban Barbie, but Barbie is silent, because, you know, she's a doll. But, you know, I'm, like, alive."

 ALEXIA

"The beauty is definitely worth the money."

 KIM

The OFFICIAL "SINGING" DOLL

ADDITIONAL
Fashions*
hold separately

Kim
Zolciak

INCLUDES:

MICROPHONE and **CD** for
"TARDY for the PARTY"
playback performances!

COLLECTIBLE
WIGS
COMING SOON!

"Now I have, thanks to Sheree, the

Can't-Snatch-It-Off-Wig."

 KIM

"A wig does not count as a hat, honey."

 PHAEDRA

"Is your wig squeezing your brain **too tight, heifer?"**

 **NENE** *(to Kim)*

"How does NeNe deal with **all that glue** on her head?"

 KIM

"Don't look at me, don't talk to me. You and your wig—get out of my life."

 **NENE** *(to Kim)*

"**Bitch,** you have **fake hair** too!"

 KIM *(to Sheree)*

"I'm a Botox junkie."

 TAMRA

"On the operating table, the doctor said,
'I should have listened to you, because you have
beautiful breasts.'"

CAMILLE
(on her now ex-husband's request that she get a boob job)

"I don't know, but I think the devil would love to hump 700 ccs."

TAMRA

*(on Alexis's boobs,
and whether they will
help keep the devil out
of Alexis's marriage)*

"It's very few and far between that you find anybody— especially here in Orange County— that has anything real, let alone boobs."

___

⬤ | GRETCHEN

"Do you know someone with

JEANA *(to all-natural Gretchen)*

real boobs?"

"I feel like **my face has fallen** and **it can't get up.**"

LYNNE
*(before
going under
the knife)*

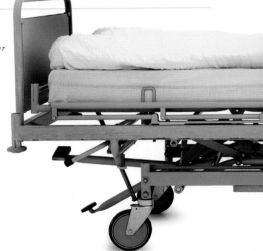

The Golden
STILETTO
A W A R D S

The Finest Achievements in
SAYING, WEARING, and DOING IT
in Real Housewives Style

THE DON'T-SELL-YOURSELF-SHORT AWARD

Camille Grammer

"I have this Jesus complex, I think. I have this need that I want to help people."

The Golden STILETTO

THE WAY-TO-KILL-THE-MOMENT AWARD

Vicki Gunvalson

For interrupting the renewal of her vows to Donn with the specs of the ring he was about to receive.

MOST PRUDENT BREAST REDUCTION

NeNe Leakes

*"I was a double D and didn't feel
the need to wear a bra."*

MOST SHAMELESS PRODUCT PROMOTION

Bethenny Frankel

*For riding around town in her
Skinny Girl Margarita car.*

MOST INSPIRED LINGUISTIC MASHUP

Kandi Burruss

*"Bougie and ghetto at the
same time?: boughetto."*

THE MOST CHECKED-OUT HOSTESS AWARD

Cristy Rice

For not just hiring a chef to cook for her guests, but hiring a chef who used a Crock-Pot and prepared foods.

BEST IMPERSONATION OF A CARTOON VILLAIN

Allison Dubois

Camille Grammer's psychic, e-cigarette-smoking friend.

THE TOMATO/TOMAHTO AWARD

Michaele Salahi

Who somehow waited until the D.C. reunion to confirm the correct pronunciation of her name.

BEST FIGHT SCENE

Sheree and Kim

THE WIG-PULLING INCIDENT

*Runner-up: Sheree and party planner Anthony,
AKA "Boo."*

BEST MISPRONUNCIATION

Ramona Singer

"KA-DOOZ"
(AKA "Kudos.")

THE QUICKEST BACKTRACK AWARD

Kim Zolciak

*For claiming she had cancer, and then
denying she had cancer about a minute later.*

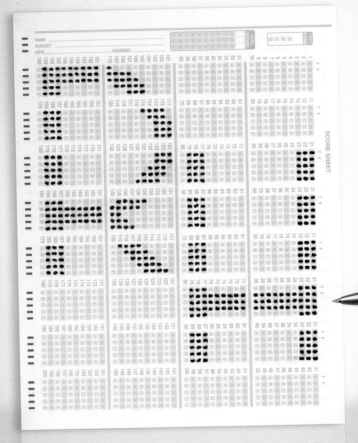

HOUSEWIVES IQ

with the Following Quizzes

Real Housewives of Orange County

You say you can't look away from the happenings in the O.C.—but did you? Test your Orange County IQ with this totally awesome quiz!

1 | Vicki hosts a sleepover and Alexis reveals she won't be able to spend the night, due to husband Jim's lack of experience caring for the kids. A shocked Tamra asks, "Do you have to go home if the kid _____?"

☐ **A. Cried**

☐ **B. Pooed**

☐ **C. Spit up**

☐ **D. Won't eat its veggies**

2 | Lynne's take on seeing herself on television: "I think I look big on TV. I look like a _____ or something like that."

☐ **A. Wrestler**

☐ **B. Whale**

☐ **C. Man**

☐ **D. Fat lady**

3 | At Tamra's "Naked Wasted" dinner party, her son Ryan makes the moves on Gretchen. She tells him, "I'm just like _____. That's why you like me."

☐ **A. A model**

☐ **B. Cameron Diaz**

☐ **C. Your ex**

☐ **D. Your mother**

---

4 | Complete these words of wisdom from Vicki: "Anyone who says money doesn't matter must be _____."

☐ **A. Stupid**

☐ **B. Drunk**

☐ **C. Poor**

☐ **D. Lazy**

Real Housewives of New York City

The Countess can't help you with this kind of class. Find out if you're at the top of the heap by taking this little Big Apple quiz!

1 | During her Scary Island dinner meltdown Kelly remarks, "Oh my god it's a witch hunt. It's like freakin' _____ in here."

☐ **A. The Crucible**   ☐ **C. Salem**

☐ **B. The Inquisition**   ☐ **D. Hades**

2 | Sonja critiques one of her outfits saying, "Look at this. What kind of guys can you pick up with _____?"

☐ **A. A chipped manicure**   ☐ **C. A one-inch heel**

☐ **B. A hunting scarf**   ☐ **D. A turtleneck**

3 | Speaking of Jill's outfit the evening of her Saks party, Ramona says, "Jill's dress that night reminded me of _____."

☐ **A. Her apartment**   ☐ **C. A Halloween costume**
☐ **B. Lady Gaga**   ☐ **D. A sofa**

---

4 | Following a fashion-show showdown with LuAnn, Bethenny states, "I need _____."

☐ **A. A gun**   ☐ **C. A time-out**
☐ **B. A cookie** ☐ **D. A box of wine**

Real Housewives of Atlanta

Think the Atlanta Housewives are just peachy?
Find out how well you know these unbe-weavable
Southern belles with this quiz!

1 | Things get heated between Kim and Lisa at Atlanta's season
one reunion, moving Lisa to say, "You need _____."

☐ **A. Medication**   ☐ **C. To get a life**

☐ **B. A beatdown**   ☐ **D. To apologize**

2 | Speaking her mind as always, NeNe says, "I really do
believe that _____ make you go crazy."

☐ **A. Other women**   ☐ **C. Blonde wigs**

☐ **B. Kids**   ☐ **D. Boob jobs**

3 | Assessing her physique, Sheree states, "I have the body of a _____."

☐ **A. Professional dancer**   ☐ **C. Movie star**

☐ **B. Hot 25-year-old**   ☐ **D. Cougar**

---

4 | Discussing the planning of her baby shower, Phaedra says, "The _____ at the shower was my idea. I don't think people celebrate the arts quite enough."

☐ **A. String quartet**   ☐ **C. Caricaturists**

☐ **B. Poets**   ☐ **D. Ballerinas**

Think you love, love, love the Jersey Housewives? Test your knowledge of the ladies from the Garden State with this quiz on who said what when.

1 | When Danielle realizes Kim G. is not as loyal as she thought, she says, "Kim G. showed her true colors, and it was a huge display of _____."

☐ **A. Low character**

☐ **C. Disgusting**

☐ **B. Deceit**

☐ **D. Betrayal**

2 | The ladies head to Atlantic City for some time away, but the Giudice daughters miss their momma. When Joe calls with a crying kid on his hands, Teresa suggests, "Give her a _____ or something."

☐ **A. Candy bar**

☐ **C. Teddy bear**

☐ **B. Lip gloss**

☐ **D. Headband**

3 | Dina reveals her secret to staying calm, saying, "There's some people that take Xanax in their life. I take a little dose of _____."

☐ **A. Chianti**

☐ **C. Valium**

☐ **B. Yanni**

☐ **D. Zen Jen**

4 | The Jersey crew piles into some gondolas on its trip to Venice, but Jacqueline is disappointed: "The gondolas were cool, but our gondola guy didn't even _____."

☐ **A. Sing**

☐ **C. Have a striped shirt on**

☐ **B. Steer**

☐ **D. Help me get in the boat**

Real Housewives of D.C.

Are you plastic or fantastic? VIP or NFI?
Prove your D.C. Housewives expertise with
this official quiz.

1 | When discussing Michaele and Tareq's appearance at the White House state dinner, Cat describes the couple as "NFI" or _____.

☐ **A. Needy Foolish Interlopers**

☐ **C. Not F*%#ing Invited**

☐ **B. Non-functioning Idiots**

☐ **D. Not Fancy or Influential**

2 | Mary recalls the only time she'd seen Michaele apart from her husband was:

☐ **A. At an aerobics class**

☐ **C. At the plastic surgeon**

☐ **B. Behind the counter at Nordstrom selling makeup**

☐ **D. At a Junior League meeting**

3 | At the D.C. reunion, Michaele defines the verb "to Salahi" as:

☐ **A. To annoy**   ☐ **C. To network**

☐ **B. To charm**   ☐ **D. To crash**

---

4 | Following the Salahis' attendance at the White House state dinner, Lynda describes the couple as "_____" in overdrive.

☐ **A. Bonnie and Clyde**   ☐ **C. Caesar and Cleopatra**

☐ **B. Heidi and Spencer**   ☐ **D. Boris and Natasha**

Real Housewives of Beverly Hills

To you, the Housewives of Beverly Hills are the biggest stars in Hollywood. Prove that you like them—you really like them!—by acing this quiz.

1 | Talking about her friend Kyle, Lisa says, "Every time she finds _____ she acts like she's found the cure for cancer."

☐ **A. A sample sale**

☐ **C. Her keys**

☐ **B. A new handbag**

☐ **D. A diamond ring**

2 | When Adrienne says, "Guess what? That's what I think most married couples do," what is she referring to?

☐ **A. Competing**

☐ **C. Having affairs**

☐ **B. Having kids**

☐ **D. Bickering**

3 | What is Camille talking about when she says, "They get in the way"?

☐ **A. Kids**
☐ **C. Her breasts**
☐ **B. Pets**
☐ **D. Other women**

4 | In preparation for her 69-mile bike ride, Kyle says "my cycling coach told me that I have to have _____."

☐ **A. A romantic dinner with Mauricio**
☐ **C. A massage**
☐ **B. An extreme bikini wax**
☐ **D. A long bath the night before**

Real Housewives of Miami

So you say you're hot for the spicy ladies of *The Real Housewives of Miami*? Find out if you're truly *caliente* or mostly *muy frio* with this quick Sunshine State quiz.

1 | Marysol offers this opinion when discussing the ongoing effort to look your best: "I'm anti-_____ until it gets really, really bad."

☐ **A. Exercise**   ☐ **C. Diet**

☐ **B. Plastic surgery**   ☐ **D. Waxing**

2 | Describing her personality, Adriana warns, "Don't dare me to do something _____, because it's like second nature to me."

☐ **A. Dangerous**   ☐ **C. Fun**

☐ **B. Stupid**   ☐ **D. Illegal**

3 | Reflecting on her responsibilities, Alexis determines the following: "If reincarnation exists, I want to come back as _____."

☐ **A. A man**

☐ **C. A dog**

☐ **B. A bird**

☐ **D. A nun**

---

4 | Larsa has this piece of advice on keeping a marriage together: "When a husband lets his wife manage _____, he's never going anywhere."

☐ **A. The bedroom**

☐ **C. The kids**

☐ **B. His career**

☐ **D. The money**

Score:

7 or fewer correct: You call yourself a *Real Housewives* fan, heifer? Someone's playing fast and loose with the truth, now aren't they? Don't worry: There's always room for redemption in the *Housewives* universe. Just wait until next season!

8 to 14 correct: You're a little tardy to the party, but not enough to get kicked out. Hit the gym a little more, get a new 'do, and adjust your attitude, and you'll be a Real Housewife expert in no time!

1.D 2.B 3.A 4.D | **ATL** 1.A 2.C 3.B 4.D | **NJ** 1.C 2.B 4.A | **BH** 1.B 2.D 3.C 4.B | **MIAMI** 1.B 2.C 3.A 4.D

15 to 21 correct: The *Real Housewives* force is strong in you. You can surely rock a weave, bring some bling, and most likely have some espionage training. Have we mentioned how cute you look today?!

22 to 28 correct: Um, congrats? It would seem you have watched every *Real Housewives* episode ever. The good news: You're not alone, and you're in good company. The bad news: It looks like you could use a little sun.

PHOTO CREDITS

ACKNOWLEDGMENTS

Thanks to the team at **BRAVO MEDIA**: Kristen Andersen, Christian Barcellos, Cameron Blanchard, Frances Berwick, Victoria Brody, Andrew Cohen, Courtney Fleischman, Shari Levine, Maile Marshall, Lauren McCollester, Kim McDade, Suzanne Park, Dave Serwatka, Ellen Stone, Trez Thomas, Jennifer Turner, Emily Yeomans, Lauren Zalaznick.

Thanks also to Matt Anderson, Melissa Bloom, James Davis, Nina Diaz, Scott Dunlop, Kathleen French, Bryan Hale, Jennifer O'Connell, Lenid Rolov, Dave Rupel, Peter Tartaglia, Rebecca Toth Diefenbach, Steven Weinstock and our fantastic production crews from Evolution, Shed Media, True Entertainment and Sirens Media.

MELCHER MEDIA would like to thank Paul Kepple and Ralph Geroni of **HEADCASE DESIGN**, Mimi O'Connor, Richard Petrucci, Susan Van Horn, everyone at **CHRONICLE BOOKS** (especially Laura Lee Mattingly, Christine Carswell, Jennifer Tolo Pierce, and Michelle Clair), and David E. Brown, Daniel del Valle, Cheryl Della Pietra, Lauren Nathan, Austin O'Malley, Katherine Raymond, Julia Sourikoff, and Megan Worman.

President and Publisher: Charles Melcher
Associate Publisher: Bonnie Eldon • *Editor in Chief:* Duncan Bock
Production Director: Kurt Andrews

Senior Editor: Holly Dolce • *Project Manager:* Shoshana Thaler

...elift Fantasy!

Lux
Boutique

PRICE

356
124
450
340

O.C. Magic

Yo...

SALES

QUANT	ITEM	PRICE
25	Prince... amond Necklace	625
1	Christ... Louboutin Pumps	865
4	Blond... ve	678
1	Diamo... ng	2,788
1	Louis... ton Luggage	1,200
2	Chinc... Fur Wrap	566
1	Louis... ton Doggie Carrier	625
1	Chan... ts	876
1	Exte... s	345
1	Gold... Tinsel	224
2	Role... ch	2,466

TOTAL

$315,625.00

ITEM

Botox
Champag...
Masseuse...
Mani-Ped...

CARD AM...

TOTAL

$...56.00

Book y...

VILLA
BIANCA

... TY with us!

Pinot Noir
...sar Salad
...et Mignon

TOTAL

CARD AMO...

Glitter Headba...
Zebra Pumps   123.86
Cheetah Tights
Leopard Print...

ITEM   4349/1017378

Glitt...

...your next BOTOX PARTY with us!

Jersey...

Posh Bou...

$589.00